Something Grazes Our Hair

Something Grazes Our Hair

Poems by S. J. Marks

University of Illinois Press

Urbana and Chicago

Publication of this work was supported in part by grants from the National Endowment for the Arts and the Illinois Arts Council, a state agency.

Library of Congress Cataloging-in-Publication Data

Marks, S. J.
    Something grazes our hair : poems / by S.J. Marks.
      p.   cm.
    ISBN 0-252-06181-0 (pbk. : alk. paper)
    I. Title.
PS3563.A668S6   1991
811'.54—dc20   90-44637
                                   CIP

Acknowledgments

Putting together these poems could not have been done without Steve Berg's and Charlie Williams's encouragement, thoughtfulness, perception, and love.

Sometimes a person touches our lives with a kindness and tenderness no one else has; such a person for me was the late poet Richard F. Hugo.

I would like to thank the Pennsylvania Council on the Arts for a grant to help me write this book.

Certain of these poems have appeared, sometimes in slightly different form, in the following journals:

The American Poetry Review: "Overnight, 1961," "Early One Sleepless," "Happiness," "To Go through Life Is to Walk across a Field," "Poem with Two Seasons Right Now," "To the Ocean," "November Woods," "Returning in Wind and Drizzle to My Home," "Near McNeil Point," "Late at Night," and "Zen Sequence"; *Cafe Solo:* "Sickness"; *Choice:* "Before the End of Summer"; *Cimarron Review:* "Not for Me"; *Colorado State Review:* "There" and "Dreaming"; *December:* "In"; *Denver Quarterly:* "Spain's Forgotten Forest"; *Existential Psychiatry:* "Orchids"; *Friday:* "In Philadelphia at Two Different Times and on the Olympic Peninsula," "Snow Squalls," and "My Mother Playing Chopin and Dying"; *The Greenfield Review:* "I'm Sick," "Starved," and "Jews"; *The Iowa Review:* "Cherries," "Tell Me," and "Something Grazes Our Hair"; *Journal of Poetry Therapy:* "Last One Out"; *The Midwest Quarterly:* "What Dreams in the Deepest Sleep" and "Russia"; *The New Yorker:* "How" and "At the State Mental Hospital"; *The North American Review:* "Thinking" and "Loneliness"; *The Painted Bride Quarterly:* "Nothing More"; *Poetry Northwest:* "Reading Charlie's Poems"; *Rundy's Journal:* "What Some People Say"; *Transpacific:* "Killing"; *Washington and Jefferson Literary Journal:* "Pond"; and *The Westigan Review:* "Summer Still Life."

"Cold Places," "To Go through Life Is to Walk across a Field," and "November Woods" will appear in *Beneath a Single Moon: Legacies of Buddhism in Contemporary American Poetry,* edited by Kent Johnson and Craig Paulenich, Shambhala Publications.

"Zen Sequence" (in a longer version) was published as a limited edition chapbook by The Wooden Spoon Press, May 1990.

For Janice Engler Marks, for her love and compassion,
for our daughters, Sasha and Lauren,
and for the journey we've had together

———————

To abolish hope is to bring thought back to the body.

Albert Camus

A lifetime burning in every moment.

T. S. Eliot

"Bits and pieces of straightforward mind" means all the bits and pieces moment after moment are straightforward mind. Not only one or two pieces, but all bits and pieces.

Dōgen

Contents

Something Grazes Our Hair

Near McNeil Point

for Bill Kulik

You need the dark for this.

Our wives and children
in the chilly sea
splashing,

harbor seals surfacing, rolling,
seabirds calling from the water.

Dusk falls
deepening the dark of the trees,
softening the edges of the shadows,
covering the islands minute by minute
until their outlines lose substance.
Only the slender
silver and black birches stand on their own.
The air, even at this hour, isn't still,
but fills with the wind's vibration.

The silence now seems to possess the presence of something palpable.
It begins and I'm not ready.
Colors—scarlets, deep lavender—
are drawn into the vast stillness.
Time
holds no meaning—
it's the sound of endlessness,

the scents of life forgotten until now.
I look at the luminous night-deep eyes of the women,

a movement of chill air
touches my skin,
and wakes me a little.

You can't look anywhere else, there is nowhere else.

Waiting

Seeking relief from the blackness of words,
I imagine you, I anticipate you,
but you never arrive. Waiting
is an act of life. Pessimistic, affable,
Beckett says he began writing because
all else failed.

        We wait
for a fate that never arrives,
a faith that remains unfulfilled.
Meanings elude. A wall of people face you—
you can't look out or find air. We miss
parts of character when they're cut,
but those lost aspects still hang there,
like ghosts.
Listen, there's Chekhov's unheard music.

I love to grapple with people who're
sulky, sullen, entirely self-absorbed.
"I was so lost, I didn't know where to begin.
It's terrifying. You can see yourself losing everything."
The final line's punctuated by
deafening blasts.
Its ferocious intensity
penetrates
like a stab wound.

A Place Where I Do Not Even Know Where I Am

The brown fields snow over.

My raging impotence to find answers,
suffocating and as inarticulate
as the scream of a dying rabbit;
the succeeding instants
without knowledge or hope.

To contemplate with savage and invulnerable
curiosity desolation
in what direction and how far or from where?

I don't know what I will need to do, but when the time comes
I'll do it or I won't.

The long moments gather themselves
and turn
on the fierce drowsing of my solitude,

and my life is past,

but too deep, too ingrained; I'm not yet able
to think it into words.

Fall

I'm going for a walk.
Janice Engler Marks

You walk, leaves fall all around you,
you walk, the crows go crazy,
you walk, the wind whistles through branches.

The exuberance of your body—
where your soul is.

The hard days fall endlessly,
honey from a spoon,

and there's no one here to tell you
you've crushed me.

Rain at Dusk

Now, the day moves out—
wind whispers and melts in the dusk.
Words, names fall away.

Weather's always surprising.
You raise the shade and look out
at the clear gray rain.

And that's the way it is
between us.
We say things to each other
to cause pain.
In this quiet room,
surprised, I feel
the rain
between us.

The Dream You Drift into as You Fall Asleep

You park your car under a willow that hides it
from the dim red twilight in a pool of darkness.

You look into your mind and see nothing but darkness.

Rocks, stacked stone slabs, dry wind,
clumps of weeds, tall grasses.

The twilight fades to full dark now,
only a flush of rose in the west.

The sore never heals.

The life wind is already blowing out of you.

Two Poems from Frenchman's Bay

I

Rain hangs in the air.

Fog runs off the water, swarming back
through the white birches and the white pines
of the bay islands.

Everyone needs protection from what they don't know.

I stand on the porch; the air slides past my face.

We're absorbed into the things
we're afraid of—
shadows, quiet, the dark.

It's all loss,
people just disappear.
Everything, everybody,
disappears into the darkness nothing
ever comes out of.

I feel your heart beating.
The room smells of rain.

II

It is the sound of sleep—it puts you at ease.

The air begins a low covering sibilance
like the night expiring.

You're inside something you can't find a way out of,
you're ready now to hear what
you should.

No one cares.

I thought I could live without you.

Burn What You Write

Red clouds rise in the afternoon.

Another wasted minute
drifts over the rooftops.

You fall asleep and dream you dream
my footsteps on the sidewalk, going away.

I'll die alone, sad,
tearing a brief hole in the air.

Spain's Forgotten Forest

Cortez, Balboa, Pizarro came from here.

A memory of an older wilder Europe.

The bitter cold hours before dawn.

Purple light,
freezing mist, shadows.
Extremadura —
a remnant of woodlands, old cork oaks
and stone oaks.
Short-toed and
Imperial eagles soar over the land
carrying prey.
Black storks in the rocky gorges;
after 1939, Republicans hid there.
Old undisturbed forests
with streams and pools.
Wolves,
griffin vultures gathering at carcasses,
and ravens.
Grass snakes and ladder snakes,
golden orioles, azurewings, bee-eaters,
madronas — strawberry trees.
Frost, rain, parching sun —
the stony ground
comes to life
with
wild lavender.

As dusk falls,
a female hawk takes a mole cricket
from her mate;

flocks of cranes against the last light,
genets, nightstalkers,
wild boars rooting for acorns.

Extremadura: the past.

Poem

He saw the colors of late October.
The woods washed with pale
lavender.
In the failing light,
he wanted to run and shout and hit people.
Something unexpected, terrifying, exhilarating,
something he'd never done before—
"It came alive when we stood in the field. . . . "

His hands were chapped and they hurt.
That's all there is to it.
"I can't tell you what I know," he wrote.
"I hold your body."
There was no one there.
He was aware of breathing in the cold air,
then he disappeared in the darkness of the trees.

Late at Night

1

I like the dull winter evenings around here—
snow, occasional fog, silence,
nothing outside but the chaos of white flakes.
Restless, weary, I stay up.

If you were awake,
I'd talk about living and dying—
there's no other conversation.

2

Sometimes, it's right here:
how people strangle from their swollen longings,
the heart giving out. Each of us lives out our fate:
how we suffer those we're attached to
is who we are.
We live in death, infected by love.

3

I want to touch everything.
It takes no time at all to become tender.
Sex, rocks—
the distinctness with which things come before me,

the more literal, the more mysterious.

4

You've gone.

The small creek, its source no one knows where,
splashes against the stones.

Leaving comes suddenly
and the startled heart bursts with a nauseous ache.

Wanting to forget hurts more.

We fear parting when we meet,
we believe when we part we'll meet again.

The sad smoke of these words curls around your silence.

5

Lying in bed, sleepless, I trace
your nose, your lips, the soft curve of your cheek,
I rub out the slight smile that hovers around your eyes.
When everyone's asleep, I want to sing
"Crazy, I'm crazy for feeling so lonely,"
but I don't.
Wind flutters the papers next to the bed.

Your face, your voice, your secret smell.
I want to write about your things as they are.
Your clothes, earrings,
even the jagged rocks where your lilies grow.

6

To cry openly. To cry the deep lake of sadness inside you.
To cry your dream. To cry in grocery stores
before shelves, cans, boxes, even when someone stops you to say,
"You're crying, can I help you?"
"No, I'm all right, I've had a great loss,
thank you," and you go on with your shopping. To mourn
people's kindness and the greenness of plants.

To open the springs of tears. To soak your cheeks.
To flood the sidewalks and streets.

To go to church crying. To celebrate family birthdays crying.
To cross Connecticut and New York and New Jersey crying
and come here.

To talk to me crying. To grieve whatever you're doing
and not stop until you're ready. To cry deeply.
To cry with your nose and eyes and belly. To weep
through your navel and cunt and asshole.

To weep of love, of tediousness, of happiness. To cry in your dress,
in the wind, in your thinning aging skin. To weep from your heart.
To weep all through insomnia and sleep and all through the day.

7

Slow despair in pitch-black night
eases the tears out of my eyelids.
Taste of moist petals
intoxicates the dry mouth
with freshness—
my naive happiness in losing my way
and finding your lips.
Are you aware of how sad, and annoyed, and happy
you've made me?

8

My mother's heart,
that pumping in the dark regions,
that drum in my head,
that pulsing I feel in the rhythms of the earth—

neither day nor night exist.
"Be gentle with women, be sensitive to them,"
that dark beating in the blood,
your heart resounds like the ocean.

I was your flesh and your stranger.

I hear the sun in your flow—
that throb of adventure,
the earth blazes with heat.
Outside, everything's you—
fingernails, voices, the cold, the days,
the lilacs, green grapes, the light, forgetfulness.

9

Your name's smooth, bright, green
like a long naked blade of prairie cordgrass.
In the air, it's sharpened like the air,
in the water, it's grooved like the current.

What we know disappears—buildings
crumble or are torn down, dirt accumulates
between the nails and boards. What
does it matter? No flowers

left in the yards. Even the stones rot.
The ache of people gone.

Politicians come with their noise, their promises,
their gestures, but the hate and fear stay.

Living's of use, despite these useless words.

10

The infinite's now. Let me say it
differently—last night
I dreamt I was starting a journey.
Today is its end.

The inadequacies of my careful language—
the intimacy of your forehead's light,
your body's unending mysteriousness,
the process of your life placed in words.

Watching you sleep next to me,
you give me a part of your life you don't have.

Quietly, I see you again, always,
for the first time, time broken, with me,
without me.

How

How can I tell you
how I need our bitter
weary chance meeting of life?

In the fading light of evening
this sadness will dissolve.
Then you are left with yourself
and the dark-eyed water of morning.

Ice sheathes the stalks.
The bleached herbs of the field are frost.
A few blackberry vines shine like blood.

It snows. I wait.
The noise of snow falling on stones and of air falling on trees
is the same.
The air loosens.

I hear the silence of night. I hear what is unsaid.
It is summer within, it is the coughing of a crow—
crow calling to crow. I hear when he calls.

A few weeds and dry leaves lift above the white surface.
It is as if I have come to an open window.

Loneliness

If you are afraid of loneliness, don't marry.
Chekhov

Late this afternoon I fell back into the word,
into the heart of the blossom.
Now I feel it quietly circling me
like a pond
as I sink down.
My eyes open in a young night
and see all things
in their secret conditions.
Darkness swallows the day
like me.

Where is the dream
that shares us?
Didn't I hear you say you had seen once
a coldness gathering in my face?

Something edges close to me
and I can only watch the blue limb, in silence,
wondering if it will open its body
and hide me.

Cherries

I am lying here alone in the dark house
and where you are you are putting out the light,
and it is evening.

Your face, quiet with dreams,
the small mouths of sleep—
I watch you with quiet trembling,
and what I feel for your softness
comes back.

Between your eyelids,
the dreams open their eyes like
rotted cherries,
and when you die, I will not know it.
Always the wind blows. We speak
to make ourselves remember.

Thinking

What you said last week before leaving
stays with me.
Now your letter says
you are far in the North.
Outside, lilacs shiver
in the April wind,
and what I cannot say stains
a thousand white birches.
Will the evening break and be joined together again?
Think of your white body,
think of the white pages, your pale lips,
this wind blowing everywhere.
In the air stars hang
and what remains of the night.
Another wind is not here yet.
Something inside me grieves
and opens.
The old houses have no ending,
their lights blink.
Since I have shut myself in this room,
how many times has the lilac flowered
and how many times the moon phased?

Before the End of Summer

When we were waiting,
I lived in a room along
the hall, and I saw inside
my eyelids at night. An
open skull, claw hands,
sparse hair, dying skin.
We ate bread with lumps
of unbaked flour and blackberry jam.
Always hungry,
sometimes we stole.
She was a dark
girl, with a pointed face.
What would happen?
She couldn't know.
I dreamed of food: ham,
turkey, rhubarb.
She dreamed of beetles.
And woke
to waiting. Nothing
came from anywhere for her.
I had plans. We did not talk.
Her dark eyes
watched me, I thought,
and I looked away.

Pond

Evening and the falling flowers of the dogwood
make shadows, and through them
the water
gives back your eyes.

I know myself touched in your heart,
your face pale.
Suddenly, a ripple colors,
a pike jumps to the surface,
becomes a glazed purple dish,
the pebbles sleep,
the eyes of an ancient beast float on the sky.

The soft pink blossoms are falling on
your hands at the edges of your life,
and my mind, tired, dark,
is touched softly at the surface.

Orchids

The moon rises
over the evening mist.
Quail crouch
in the quiet grasses—
something lies inside me
without words.
The *tchee tchee* of the quail echo from cliff walls.
Leaves, orchids are on fire in the mountains.
Where should I look for you?

The shadow of my father's plum tree on the window
fills me with pain.

The smiling nightflowers open like a mist.

Dreaming

Between us now the long wheatfields
lie in the heavy wind, gray, brown
under the frozen weather, dark in the sleep
of those who have gone away.

Now, in December, we go through so easily
that we don't feel the distance, but the fields
everywhere we look for or remember
bend like my arms.

Being here, I know that the fields are dead.
Older and slower, I walk the streets.
The evening washes my skin.
I think of you. The field is a dream.

It stitches me with distance
like a wound. It is
the rising and falling of my breath,
long and harsh as the icy wind.

Summer Still Life

I am writing a tired silence,
a leaf that rots without falling.

I have wasted this night three times.

You will go on, whatever I say,
this is the end of it.

Where the Shadows Lie

He can't make out the line between night sky and sea,
he feels the darkness inexplicably wedged between his ribs
(those smudges of bone), shadows in other shadows,
a nightbird pecks at the back of his right hand.
He feels nothing, only himself.

His bones ache inside his skin —
so sore he can feel them all;
the tips of his fingers are numb.

And these words have taken us this far,
your warm soft presence
next to me —
nothing but space.

I want to be as close to you as I can
for as long as I can.

We don't expect happiness from each other,
just each other.

Derelicts

We're all becoming the past.

What we are and what we think we are
are two different things. Discovering
who one is hurts.

There's something about the guilt of character,
something about establishing harmony with your past,
something about having the courage to come back
to the center of your past and face it.

Something beautiful about loving somebody
but not being capable of loving fully
because of your not having reconciled the past.

You always stretch the limits,
to see how close you can go to death and still be alive,
how much you can dare as a human
without killing yourself.

The real meaning of their life is they keep going;
the act of going is more important than where.

"I feel like nothing of this world belongs to me."

Something loves us and torments us.

Where there's silence and absolute calm,
what have we to do
with passionate words?
They make no sense at all.

The moments fly by and we talk.
I sit, and, in laziness and confusion,
don't know what to do with my hands.

Once, when I was a boy,
I watched a girl swim,
and, knowing nothing of love,
I felt mysterious desire.
Something inside of me groaned.

Years pass. Under the knife of
our own sadness,
something in us breaks,
falls to pieces,
and what we attain is a kind of
inexpressible calm.

Cold Places

The sound of the hard wind
pummels the pines and cedars
and brings the sound of approaching winter,

it comes through a rift left by a sudden emptiness in my heart.

The heaviness of aging presses on us,
a loneliness, sadness;
you're sleeping—you know nothing of what's happening.

The whole of the evening's light
is sucked into the silver maple;
the inside of the tree warms with it.

That distant sound is the thunder of winter.

I see your nipples,
large, swollen and dark,
I hear the first drops of night rain
spatter the window.

What flows behind my eyelids now
is the deep current of life,
it's what we have
to help us remember that no matter where we are
we are together.

Your sleeping face soft in the gentle light—
nothing's more beautiful than your young face
in its sleep.
Straining my ears, I think I hear
faint late-autumn wind blowing down across the hill
behind the house. Warm breath
from your parted lips comes to my face,
the dim light from the lavender bedroom walls flows down
inside your mouth. Your round, high breasts

fit in the palm of my hand. I lean
to take them in my mouth.

Regrets flow in me and out—
your glowing skin and scent are forgiveness.

The sound goes on and on—informing me of the cold;
inside and out, withered leaves still cling to the branches.

To Go through Life Is to Walk across a Field

How delicious to walk into the stillness—
the mist surrounds us, we sink into the tall wild grasses,
the meadows blur in the heat,
the edge of the sky's purple.

You're dozing—you're not asleep, but dreaming
you're longing for sleep.

I'd like to know
what will happen in the rest of my life.
Gulph Creek cuts through the valley.

I remember the people in Chekhov saying good-by,
"We shall never see each other again."

The wind's everywhere—
in the trees, in the rain, in the house, in this poem,
in death, everywhere.

In the evening light
the maple tree glows red.
I feel the warmth of your hands.

The birches, the street, our faces lit
by a car's headlights.

Home now,
the sound of rain
down the drainpipe.

I came to you because
suffering warms the coldness of life.

Poem with Two Seasons Right Now

What there is of it,
this heartache continues.

I go out and play racquetball—
smashing the small blue viciously hard regulation racquetball
with fanatical cuts and drives and slams,
beating and slashing at it in hatred for the blind strength of the wall itself.
Sweating it out.

Nothing fills the spaces.

It is like this—
this autumn when the grass
has a thick silken green.
I go through life
as life seems to want me to.

When the wind stops,
I don't notice the great quiet
that comes over the field.
What I hear is a young woman patient,
anguished and despairing over her life and the murder
of her cousin—
the number 1 ranked welterweight in the world—
say, "Nobody promises you tomorrow."

And now this—
you dream while frozen lilac twigs
clap at your storm windows.
You have been left here holding someone
when there is no one anymore to hold.

In Philadelphia at Two Different Times and on the Olympic Peninsula

In my house on North Fifteenth Street,
I look from a second-floor window
at the half-filled footprints I made
in the snow coming in.

I can see myself on a trail high up in the Washington Olympics
between heavy smooth white snowbanks; I stride along,
hardly aware of what I'm doing.
The cold air takes all my breath. I stop—
the smell of pines, just now in view; sweat
from under my armpits slides down my ribs.

Manya, my seventy-eight-year-old cousin, calls from New York
and tells me, "I've always been afraid
about what will happen."

Occasionally, the wind moves a branch
from a tree and snow sifts down
through sunlight. The sky is pure blue.
I hate our helplessness.

I think what I have not quite, ever, put into words before—
that any parting is painfully mysterious.

These days you look so drained, so utterly exhausted,
one hand thrown protectively across your eyes,
that I'm moved in an old way. Carefully,
I slip in beside you.

Last night, at a party, I heard you say,
"I was so touched and it was too late to tell her."
I have no idea, really, of what to do.
I put my arms around you.

In the moonlight, your gray eyes shine
and the fine line under your chin, that first line of age,

is just barely visible. You are more beautiful
now than you were ten years ago.

Outside, a strong wind has come up, the walls creak,
the windowpanes rattle.

Snow Squalls

At the end of February, there had been
two snow squalls,
the afternoon gray,
the wind so fierce I heard
branches crash in the woods,
the brief snow froze,
glazing the highways—

we were possessed
by the flawless isolation
and the numbing cold.

The woods formed by these trees
extend for acres, in places growing
very dark; to walk through it's
fearful, delightful.
From above,
in the swirl of raging wind and snow,
comes a frightening wonderful mysterious sound,
a sound as meaningful and mournful
as a life spent in solitary places,
strong, sad, clear as cold
mountain water.
White stalks visible through the windshield.
In your quiet smile, lit by bright light
coming shadowless from the North,
is more love than I have ever seen.
The drive is bordered by pines
and moss-green rocks. I don't fall asleep
without thinking of them. Frost-lined
stems and branches, brown trees,
frozen into place, caught as we creep
up the hill. The morning so bright
it's like a dream.

My Mother Playing Chopin and Dying

I have gone for a walk in the twilight.
There have been two nights of frost,
the branches are brown and black.

They operated on her for five hours;
they cut and cut, but there were too many scarlet clumps,
so they stopped and sewed her up.

Now and then she wept, but she wasn't afraid of dying,
just wept or screamed because it hurt.
She was bitter about dying so young.

I held her hands in my hands and could feel
the disease twitching her finger muscles. She clawed my arms.

If she knew what she meant, it would never
enter my head to say I miss her.

The nocturne she played tells of suppressed pain
and reveries. It is calm, clear, and moving.

For thirteen years, I've worked at these terrifying lines;
the notes, the words still hold a lot of secrets,
things I don't understand.

Sometimes, just as I'm falling asleep,
I can feel her breathing against my face when I was a child
and touching me with her hand.

I sit in that chair,
gazing at the play of light over the branches and the river.

Outside the window, everything is still
in the afternoon light, no wind, no birds.

I like to look down into the water.
It is clear and cold, and I can see
the big round stones on the bottom.

It hurts so much.

When I was little, I could feel her voice
all over my body when she spoke;
often, she was angry with me for not hearing what she said.
I was listening to her voice.

November Woods

for Masao Abe

Gray sky, mist, the trees black and wet,
branches dripping rain,
soggy ground and oak leaves under my feet.

A day of unknowing, of knowing I do not know,
a day of uncertainty,
the day of my life.

Somehow,
I breathe easier here—
in the cool damp air.

I move through the woods,
moving slowly through drizzle,
stepping carefully on the spongy wet leaf mold on the forest floor,
rain spattering the trees and fallen leaves
deadens the sound of my footsteps.

We change what yesterday did to us.
After my mother's cancer,
and my just-born daughter
dying in hours,
I can hear what is. All of what is. Whatever it is.

I walk to where you're staying,
to your class,
to hear you say these kind thoughtful words,
"You do not know what water is.
You might visit the Zen master and ask him.
He may pour the jar of water into a glass and say
by word or gesture, 'Please drink it,' " and, later, in another context,
"He may say, 'When you have none, I will take it away from you.' "

After class, you tell me you fell on the ice
and bruised your shoulder; I leave you,

and, later, my shoulder and chest ache so,
I have to take to bed and sleep.
On Zou Fulei's plum branch
spring is like breath,
it goes but has to return,
the smoky mist dies,
the empty room's cold,
this ink branch keeps its shadow on my mind.

Overnight, 1961

The pale light of daybreak—
someone's fingerprints on the cold glass door
and the barely whitening edges of the branches
are still as silver.
No one is awake,
only the electric light pants wearily,
the chill sweet odor of aluminum;
even the indistinct smell of my sweat
strikes my throat harshly.
How much worse it must be for you,
another man's wife.
You take the pillow
and put it on the rack above your head.
Suddenly, in sadness, we hold one another.
When I look out of the train,
in the mountains at an unknown place,
close to dawn now,
lilacs, the flowers of memory, are blossoming.

In

In the dry, the lonely,
in the bare trees old branches wait.
Hate and hunger move the shadows before dawn.

The winds circle,
the sapless grass stems crackle
under my feet.

My mother purses her old mouth:
just this deep sour taste of strawberries, careful words,
pain.

Sometimes, I want to go up
to you
to feel the bones of your face with my hands.

The tree in its own body cries out
also, quietly.

The leaves dry on the maples:
on my lip slowly dries
the only sign of suffering.

Sickness

The miserable wet long night of the Northwest.
The wolf's red eyes
burn in the bottom of the night.

The pale yellow moon thins and
disappears in a wink.

A crow, sleeping,
utters a throaty gurgle in the wind.

Through the narrow alleys and streets.

There is a strange bird
grieving in a voice unknown in this world.

The grass under the wind crawls like a snake.

Bare branches curl in the icy air,
a few dangling leaves sway on the twigs,
empty nests—
the tree is silent
as it dreams.

Only thick hoarfrost spreads all over the world,
only a disc of cold moon hangs on the sky.
The moon dims
as it dreams
of its own fragment.

At the State Mental Hospital

Byberry, PA

Seven o'clock, the landscape fills with cars;
patients wander through the broken cornstalks.
A man wades in mist up to his waist
like someone's ghost with no legs.

A pheasant glows in the bluish light,
drops from a branch, then flies off.
His wings take the summer.
Twenty-three black hickories stand against the sky.

Early One Sleepless

Early one sleepless
evening before a storm in
Iowa, I saw
a huge crowd of people
whose faces
were gone.

A wolf's jaws bit my heart.

Dawn falls.
The light in its eyes scares me.

Overnight, it sharpens its claws.

Hours of pleasure and grief
have worn the soft bones of light.

What Dreams in the Deepest Sleep

Its mouth open,
male-throated—

it needs the night in my body.

I feel changes in the veins
in the throat of the mountain,
the secret-keeping stones,

and I hate these words,
the grass-blade's moon,
the lakes of milky light—
part of me;

I can't tell how strange it is.

Starved

for Dick Hugo

Write it in black ink
on ordinary paper:
they had no food,
they died of hunger.
This field is so big.
Write I don't know if any survived.
The bodies have been recorded.
Nobody's here—
the air smiles, shouts, and keeps growing,
leaps into the field for emptiness to die.

We're in the field where it becomes flesh.
It remains silent like a false witness,
sunlit, green. There're trees—
bark to suck for water,
the daily ration of a view
before one goes blind. High above, a bird
moves its shadow of terrifying wings
across their mouths. Jaws open
and snap shut, tooth hard on tooth.
In the night sky, a skyraider releases
imaginary loaves.
They talk, their mouths full of earth.
Write about the stillness.

Jews

I'm left—Jews leave Russia
and iron seeps from the stems of silence.
These refugees follow a fragrance
to doorsteps in cities and in the wrists of rivers.

And I stay. There's only a mulberry tree,
my mother playing the piano.
You can't leave me, she says,
now that I'm dead and need you.

From a distance, I see the dream's red brick,
and, outside, the sick people
my grandfather, their pharmacist, is handing prescriptions to.
All these loved people lie tenderly down with me in the bed of childhood.

I'm Sick

Frosts. The street
is cold porcelain.
I'm sitting in the old house, speaking
into the silence.

I've seen no one for days.
Someone knocked
and left milk.
I don't want to die.

But I'm up and my head aches.
Things hide,
then emerge with the squelchy
sound of wet shoes
on snow.

Images:
my breath doesn't help the cloud and the old man
gazes for a long
time after the disappearing platoon,
then he starts out carefully, smokes a cigarette,
looks at a dead body lying on its back—
from the pale stomach
something unimaginable flows.
It's colder because it's night.
A young woman tries waking her dead son.

The phone keeps ringing. I don't answer it.

Russia

Snow falls in the morning twilight
on the old snow.
Frost chokes the windows. They have
not heard anyone screaming with hunger.
I've been half-awake all night.
Something darts under the shining birches.

Winter is so long. The lost faces
I never understand.
Prisoners hardened beyond grief and anger—
eyes dark, soft necks.
They suffer. Ice
forms on their eyebrows,
in their nostrils;
cloths wet with breath, and, at the
edges, crusted with ice.

The shadow of dark birds
in your eyes.

The words ache
to say I love you.
From indolence.

The prisoners are around me in the dark,
they would chew my body to the bone,
but know, as I know, I am not here.

All I have
is
the light soft as eyelids, and the snow
wiping its wet wings on the window.

Killing

I'm a child again.
I walk on flowers—
leaves and sweet blossoms. They open
among the exploding bursts of
machine guns. Now a fine mist.

Medics sew people's flesh.
Tonight,
they'll carry them
over the rice fields
in the darkness.
Flowers quietly open.

The sky burns with the color of dying.
My skin itches as if it too had been set afire.
Animal's flesh.
In their breasts, the hearts of women shrivel
and fade.

It's children who are killing for you and dying.
Are you dreaming?
I know you'll kill me tonight.

Firebombs,
the cough of guns.
And I'm alive. I can still breathe the smells: roses and dung.
When will I say the words choking me?

Tell Me

I was sitting at my desk and I heard your voice
in the bedroom. You were crying
between day and night, you were getting on a streetcar
after a long illness, you stood on a bridge over a river
that said all this is true.

Someone is kissing your sour mouth.
I'd like to fall asleep
and wake up after, when this is all over—

I forget that this is what I'm saying.
Tell me whiteness
should be the rain,
the stone,
your lips hiding words.
Tell me you don't stink of dying.

Last One Out

1.

This evening, 7:30, Friday, dusk settling in,
I'm the last one out of the clinic,
the parking lot empty as I leave.

A grueling week—
long hours, my last couple
so fearful of their vulnerabilities,
the husband, a heavy drinker,
bitter
at not being able to visit his wife, a drug user,
who has turned to her mother and sisters.
She hadn't told him
where she'd gone.
How can I help them?

I write this driving home at the end
of one of those working days
when all of my clever insights turned out to be wrong,
when I realized what to say only after the family had left,
when what I thought was clarified wasn't,
I only confused things,
my silence taken
merely as inattentiveness.

2.

These are the days
when time doesn't feel the way you once thought it would:
each moment opening and expanding, each moment the last.

I remember you afternoons;
I take you with me.
Beyond your eyes, the afternoon dies.

What cuts us off from each other
when we lose touch?
Sometimes, in my room or out here,
it comes over me like a haze,
that life isn't really happening:
it's terrifying—
I don't recognize anyone.

Family Life

I'm in Philadelphia, watching the moon slide
beyond the buildings. Janice sleeps next to me.
Cold night air brushes my face.
I remember sitting
at my grandmother's in Chicago, her knotted fingers pulling
the deep pink yarn back and forth,
her loving warmth in the silence
returns to me.
Lake Michigan rocks behind her. I can smell it—
the tangy scent of space and lost love.
She falls asleep, her fingers pressed
to her chin, her fingers touching her lips.
Dreams wrinkle her eyelids,
her mouth opens in a small circle,
she smells of sleep. Darkness
presses at the window while I wait for her to waken.

Kissing Janice while I'm still asleep,
I think she is someone else
and the unexpected touch of her lips excites me.
When I reach down to stroke her mysterious
wet place, I wake, remembering
who I am and what I see. Gentleness
and lust mingle in my head.
I'm trying to understand,
to know what happens.

Janice's arm brushes mine in her sleep. Her touch
surprises me, the way laughter amazes a baby.
I know what I love, the moon
hanging in the black sky above, lovely,
perfect, homeless, and that
I know who I am and am with.

Reading Charlie's Poems

for C. K. Williams

I've read what you said again,
slowly,
turning the pages, thinking of you,
thinking of our friendship.
I'm sad at the thought of our lives passing
and I don't want to sort the ghosts
drifting through the pages.
I give up and stare at the sentences
of your words, of yourself.
Here, your dry sight opens
Tolstoy's dark sack, the roots of doubt,
the tiny angers of the teeth,
fat birds, cannibals,
the secrets of our children's hearts.
Like a surgeon, you've dissected
nerves of the dead world.
I know how you've
sweated mornings bringing the nightmare
facts to life. Hunched over your own
guts under the glare of the electric lamp,
what you want to say makes your fingers itch,
and,
in the end, you tell yourself
it's here.
You cleanse the infection from your eyes
with words as clear as the rain
that give birth to and curse the earth.

Something Grazes Our Hair

Something grazes our hair, gets
tangled in it
and leaves.

The last light welds itself to the hand.
The light of the shadow is its milky darkness,
the light on the moon like a skin.

There are silences in the heart,
a hand
with its fingers curled up
in the palm.
And a tree. I break off
a small branch,
I touch the jagged edges
and my fingers itch.

I feel your hands in my sleep, soothing me,
trying to find out who I am.
They're taking apart something without me,
something so human
I can't even remember the dream it became
when I wake.

Happiness

It is raining this afternoon.
I live
in a house I know everything about.
All one evening I dream about you,
feeling under my fingers
the talk of lips and tongue.
You smile at me,
you know the
water which is the heart flowing in dark light.

I wake in you.

I take your face in my hands,
your hair silky and damp and glowing,
my hands stained by your blurred shadow.

Your face is
at the window
against the old trees where the light dies.

I don't care what cold might possess me.

What Some People Say

In May, the afternoon brown sets in at about five,
by six, it slides down trees and fences;
a brown darkness glazes the pavements at seven
and isolates the streetlamps and their feeble yellow glow.
In the final stage of dusk, a dark sediment
rings the lamps. Night begins.

Natalie Wood's sister, Lana, quotes her, saying,
"You know what I want? I want yesterday,"
before she died. But we're trapped in our lives,
in our time, aging, just as Natalie was.

"After the age of fifty," Julio Cortazar writes,
"We begin to die little by little in the deaths of others."
I knew it when Steve told me Dick Hugo had just been buried in Seattle,
and a part of me died too.

Mike Nichols says he's searching, always, in scripts, for what he calls
the "event"—the moment or series of moments—
that will illuminate the author's meaning,
that will reveal "real people living their lives."

And this writing, is it somehow
that immediacy, the life I feel pulsing in me today?
What I'm trying to do is write
statements of personal suffering others make
so what I say is clear—
life's hopeless but we go on anyway, love's momentary
but forever, and our lives are everything—
but we're unimportant and will be forgotten.

There

There is a sadness I feel when we touch each other—
a melancholy inside our fingers
like the small rain falling
down past the windows.
Your eyes are dark, and the thought of you moves me—
one could say as much through a stalk of grief.

You know even in the quiet of our kiss
that petals are opening in another room
as you sit across from me, talking.
If only I could touch your naked shoulder,
the rain making the same
slow sound I have been hearing all day.
And still you move me,
and what lies between us
flickers like black light.

Nothing More

When you realize you've lived most of your life,
you want to have a sudden tangible impact on people,
you want "to be that self which one truly is,"
as Kierkegaard says. Sometimes, your eyes catch
someone else's—and hold for a few moments.
When you look away,
there's a strange feeling, as if you've shed
a drab outer skin; it's old and brittle, and, as you move,
it crackles and drops off.
You breathe more deeply. The sky's
sharper. You taste the air,
you see every branch, every movement of the forest grasses
in the May breeze.

These are days you never forget,
when everything you want to happen does happen.

A simple day. Eating, touching, walking,
never enough time to say to each other
all the things that need saying; no way
to tell all that's happened to each of us
before the other appears.

We're absolutely alone—
we can deny the aloneness, but it doesn't go away.
We're in our friends' minds.
Some are trying to live and some are dying.
We're fading out of their minds.
I'm fading out of the memories of people I knew
twenty years ago. And, as they fade
out of my memory, it's as if they're dying.
Dying is forgetting. Nothing more.
You're not dead until there isn't a flash of you in memory
left anywhere.

Not for Me

In those days, I wanted you to save me.
I'd been reading Chekhov's "A Boring Story"
and I thought Katya was you.
How I longed for you to write or call me
or come to take me in tenderness.
I savor the times you greeted me
with your mouth open—wet, waiting, alive
but we're never alone now.

What I want is you,
but I can't moan or gasp on the page.
I can't describe or write
how I see and feel you.
It's how Giacometti felt
late in his life about his lover.
Sometimes, he'd watch her make love with others.
To see is to touch—
to see what he needed to see.
All of this is my failure to act.

The only thing still alive is my gaze—
it's the difference between death and me.
"The older I grow, the more
I find myself alone,"
Giacometti said. "At the last,
I shall be entirely alone . . .
knowing from experience that
everything I undertake slips
through my fingers. . . . "
There's no wisdom here.
Not for me.
But I can see you, and remember.
There's a fragment,

a moment,
a few words that say
what I know or sense, what I mean.

Returning in Wind and Drizzle
to My Home

Sea-wind and fog hover over the river's waves,
the evening's mist,
green hills suddenly fugitive, disappear.

A universe glitters, pure as ice.
Beneath the river sky, an Indian fisherman
in a short brown hunting jacket looks like a porcupine,
his boat a waterfowl. Fish
burrowing deep in winter mud escape his fishing hooks,
though a few are gilled in his nets. As he walks home,
branches along the trail bend, break; nothing to prop them.
He knocks at a gate in the night, frogs croak.
Bridge into the reservation, tied-up boats, no travelers in sight.

Lying awake here, once again,
ashamed of myself, I look at this photograph—
"Returning in wind and drizzle to my home."

Zen Sequence

for Steve Berg

It's as though
everyday life doesn't exist,
a distillation of fear, a primordial terror,
an invisible shadow,
a silence within a silence,
the shape of people's lives.

If she hadn't talked to me when I was ten . . .
I don't understand what has happened,
I wouldn't still feel her presence,
but as I move toward the age she was
I slowly understand.

*   *   *   *

Brown hills laced with fingers
of dark green. In the gathering twilight, I think
of the great silence that settles on the land;
fear and muted colors hang in me
like fragments of a collective memory.
As you watch our daughter,
your gray eyes shine like theirs with a fierce love:
I can't take my eyes from you.

Out there—terror strikes
the living things around me.
The silences and darkness deepen
through a web of leafy branches to the ground
with a sound like soft rain.

I see this picture week after week.
I drive in silence through the brief dusk and into the night,
but it's beautiful, the wind fresh from the river
carrying an iodine smell, a smell of flowers
I know by half-forgotten names.
It's a ride on the edge, among half-seen and
unseen things.

*   *   *   *

Water insects skim the brown surface of the creek.
The trees take me—
drawn into their silence,
I move through the redolent spaces like a dreamer,
the air rainwashed.

"You are as lovely as stone, and as fierce."

"I'm so deep in my loneliness,
I'm drowning."

* * * *

The blush of rouge on your cheeks
like the color of Hsu Wei's *Sixteen Flowers*.
Welcome me, take me,
I'm jealous.
The color doesn't stay fresh.
Caught on the paper
life dies,
the voices of the flowers don't sing.

*   *   *   *

Driving home,
the voices of people drift through me,
nothing is what it was:

"I like the uncertainty,
the threat of losing. . . . "

There are things I didn't tell you,
but I loved you.

*   *   *   *

Chords of a Chopin nocturne my mother played
settle on my hearing and stay.
Just a little song,
but its particles of sound are so wondrously blent
that sensing it is like tasting sweet fruit.
What makes me so happy sometimes?
Glimpses, glintings.
Something is always happening.
Still, I'm sad—it comes and I barely recognize it.
When I have time, I ask myself what it is.
It's not the same consuming soreness;
it comes and I live through it.
One closes one's heart to pity.
This continual failing of life comforts in its own way.
The eye you see it with sees you back.

To the Ocean

I am no longer sure of anything.

Perhaps,
that's what life's about—people leaving
and you learning how to live again.

You smell seaweed and iodine. You breathe the wind.

In a poem, I will explain all you must do
in order to be happy, and all you must not do.
You must know sadness.
Dreams are difficult to hold onto.

I like to delve deeply into new people—their unspoken meanings,
their secrets, their mysteries, their lies.
To pay with oneself.

People ache. They can't manage to tell
their experiences. They have nothing to give.
No words.

My outrageous appetite for living, my apparent hardness.
The sea today stings.
I forget those things I don't like
about myself. The water bears my body, conceals it, courses off it.

Regenerating me,
so I'll be able to touch the people I love
and can't do without.

I love them so much.

Even the dead.
One must let the dead live within one.

I return to life deprived of all
I thought it impossible to do without.

Poetry from Illinois

History Is Your Own Heartbeat
Michael S. Harper (1971)

The Foreclosure
Richard Emil Braun (1972)

The Scrawny Sonnets and
Other Narratives
Robert Bagg (1973)

The Creation Frame
Phyllis Thompson (1973)

To All Appearances:
Poems New and Selected
Josephine Miles (1974)

The Black Hawk Songs
Michael Borich (1975)

Nightmare Begins Responsibility
Michael S. Harper (1975)

The Wichita Poems
Michael Van Walleghen (1975)

Images of Kin:
New and Selected Poems
Michael S. Harper (1977)

Poems of the Two Worlds
Frederick Morgan (1977)

Cumberland Station
Dave Smith (1977)

Tracking
Virginia R. Terris (1977)

Riversongs
Michael Anania (1978)

On Earth as It Is
Dan Masterson (1978)

Coming to Terms
Josephine Miles (1979)

Death Mother and Other Poems
Frederick Morgan (1979)

Goshawk, Antelope
Dave Smith (1979)

Local Men
James Whitehead (1979)

Searching the Drowned Man
Sydney Lea (1980)

With Akhmatova at the Black Gates
Stephen Berg (1981)

Dream Flights
Dave Smith (1981)

More Trouble with the Obvious
Michael Van Walleghen (1981)

The American Book of the Dead
Jim Barnes (1982)

The Floating Candles
Sydney Lea (1982)

Northbook
Frederick Morgan (1982)

Collected Poems, 1930-83
Josephine Miles (1983)

The River Painter
Emily Grosholz (1984)

Healing Song for the Inner Ear
Michael S. Harper (1984)

The Passion of the Right-Angled Man
T. R. Hummer (1984)

Dear John, Dear Coltrane
Michael S. Harper (1985)

Poems from the Sangamon
John Knoepfle (1985)

Eroding Witness
Nathaniel Mackey (1985)
National Poetry Series

In It
Stephen Berg (1986)

Palladium
Alice Fulton (1986)
National Poetry Series

The Ghosts of Who We Were
Phyllis Thompson (1986)

Moon in a Mason Jar
Robert Wrigley (1986)

Lower-Class Heresy
T. R. Hummer (1987)

Poems: New and Selected
Frederick Morgan (1987)

Cities in Motion
Sylvia Moss (1987)
National Poetry Series

Furnace Harbor:
A Rhapsody of the North Country
Philip D. Church (1988)

The Hand of God and
a Few Bright Flowers
William Olsen (1988)
National Poetry Series

Bad Girl, with Hawk
Nance Van Winckel (1988)

Blue Tango
Michael Van Walleghen (1989)

The Great Bird of Love
Paul Zimmer (1989)
National Poetry Series

Eden
Dennis Schmitz (1989)

Waiting for Poppa at the
Smithtown Diner
Peter Serchuk (1990)

Great Blue
Brendan Galvin (1990)

Stubborn
Roland Flint (1990)
National Poetry Series

What My Father Believed
Robert Wrigley (1991)

Something Grazes Our Hair
S. J. Marks (1991)

The Surface
Laura Mullen (1991)
National Poetry Series